AI unlocked for New Age Students

The Smart Student's Tools

Amaara Verma & Abeer Verma

Fusion Books

Publisher : **Fusion Books**
X-30, Okhla Industrial Area, Phase-II
New Delhi-110020
Phone : 011- 40712200
E-mail : wecare@diamondbooks.in
Website : www.diamondbooks.in
Edition : 2026

AUTHOR'S NOTE

Hi! We're Abeer and Amaara.
We belong to a generation that doesn't remember a world without the internet. But now, something even bigger is shaping our lives — Artificial Intelligence.

We use AI to study, to search, to create presentations, to write, to design, and sometimes even to think. But one question kept bothering us:
Are we really understanding AI — or just using it?
This book started as conversations between us.

Abeer was curious about how AI tools actually work — how data becomes decisions, and how systems can be built better.
Amaara kept asking bigger questions — Is AI fair? Can it replace creativity? Who is responsible when AI makes mistakes?
We realized students need both perspectives.

AI is powerful.
But power without understanding is risky.
And understanding without ethics is incomplete.
This book is our attempt to unlock AI for students — not just as users, but as thoughtful creators.
Let's explore it together.

— Abeer & Amaara

Preface

We Artificial Intelligence is no longer a futuristic concept. It is part of daily student life.

From smart study apps and chatbots to recommendation systems and creative tools, AI is quietly shaping how we learn, think, and plan our futures.

Yet most students interact with AI passively. Few pause to understand:

- What AI actually is
- How it learns
- How it influences decisions
- How it can be used responsibly

AI Unlocked for New Age Students is designed to bridge that gap. This book explains AI in simple, relatable language while encouraging critical thinking. It combines practical tool guidance with ethical reflection, helping students become not just faster learners — but smarter decision-makers.

Aligned with the spirit of NEP 2020 and future-ready education, this book encourages curiosity, creativity, and accountability.
AI will not replace students.

But students who understand AI will lead the future.

Foreword

In The emergence of Artificial Intelligence marks one of the most significant transformations in human history. Unlike previous technological revolutions, AI directly influences how we think, create, and make decisions.

For students, this shift is both an opportunity and a responsibility. What makes AI Unlocked for New Age Students unique is its perspective. Written by young minds who themselves belong to the digital generation, this book bridges the gap between technology and lived student experience.

Abeer Verma brings technical curiosity and clarity to understanding how AI tools function. Amaara Verma brings reflective depth, asking the questions that ensure technology remains ethical and human-centered.

Together, they offer more than information — they offer balance. This book does not simply teach AI tools.

It encourages discernment.
It builds awareness.
It prepares students not only to use technology — but to shape it responsibly.

In a world increasingly guided by algorithms, thoughtful education is essential. This work contributes meaningfully to that goal.

INDEX

Chapter 1

What is AI? – Understanding the Basics

Learning Objectives

By the end of this chapter, you will be able to:

• Understand what Artificial Intelligence (AI) means.
• Learn the difference between AI, Machine Learning, and Deep Learning.
• Explore how AI evolved and what types of AI exist.
• Know how data and patterns play a role in AI systems.
• Identify AI tools used in daily life.

What Is AI? – The Big Question

Let's begin with a simple question: Have you ever spoken to Siri, Alexa, or Google Assistant? Ever used a chatbot to ask questions or get homework help? Or maybe you've received movie or shopping recommendations from an app that seemed to "know" you well? All of these are examples of Artificial Intelligence, or AI.

In simple words, Artificial Intelligence refers to machines or computer systems that can think, learn, and make decisions like humans—or at least try to. These systems are built to perform tasks such as understanding language, recognizing images, solving problems, and even learning from experience.

AI doesn't mean robots with feelings or human brains inside machines (like in sci-fi movies). Instead, it's mostly about software that learns from data to make smart decisions.

The 5Ws of AI: Simplified

Let's use the 5Ws framework to break it down:

What is AI?
AI is a branch of computer science that enables machines to simulate human intelligence. This includes:

- **Understanding** (language, speech, or text)
- **Reasoning** (solving problems)
- **Learning** (from experience or data)
- **Acting** (making decisions and taking action)

Why was AI created?

Humans created AI to:
- Reduce effort and automate tasks
- Make faster and smarter decisions
- Solve complex problems (like traffic, disease detection, and more)

Where is AI used?

In phones, schools, hospitals, banks, games, weather apps, maps, factories, and almost everywhere!

When did AI begin?
AI as a field was born in 1956, but became more powerful after 2000, with the rise of the internet, big data, and faster computers.

Who uses AI?
All of us! Whether we realize it or not, students, teachers, businesses, doctors, and even farmers use AI today.

AI vs Machine Learning vs Deep Learning

These three terms are often confused. Let's understand how they are related:

Term	What It Means	Example
AI	Machines that mimic human intelligence	Google Assistant
Machine Learning (ML)	A type of AI where machines learn from data instead of rules	YouTube recommendations
Deep Learning	A type of ML using brain-like structures (neural networks)	Face recognition on phones

So, AI is the big umbrella, under which Machine Learning and Deep Learning sit.

Think of it like this:
AI = Goal
ML = Way to achieve it
Deep Learning = Advanced tool for ML

A Quick History of AI

Here's a timeline of how AI grew from a science fiction dream into a real-world technology:

Year	Milestone
1956	The term Artificial Intelligence was coined at Dartmouth Conference.
1997	IBM's Deep Blue defeated world chess champion Garry Kasparov.
2011	Siri launched on iPhones.
2016	Google's AlphaGo beat a top human Go player.
2022	OpenAI launched ChatGPT, a major breakthrough in natural language AI.
2024	AI became part of India's NEP classrooms and student tools.

Types of AI: Narrow, General, and Generative

1. Narrow AI (Weak AI):
- Can perform only one task well.
- **Example:** Google Maps gives directions, but cannot write a poem.

2. General AI (Strong AI):
- Can perform any task a human can.
- Still a dream—scientists are working on this.

3. Generative AI:
- Can create something new: text, images, videos, music.
- **Example**: ChatGPT can write essays; Midjourney creates art.

Type	Human-like Thinking?	Current Use
Narrow AI	×	✓ Widely used
General AI	✓	× Not yet achieved
Generative AI	Creates content	✓ Used in education, art

How Does AI Work?

AI doesn't have a "brain" like humans. Instead, it learns from data and patterns.

Imagine feeding thousands of math problems to an AI. Eventually, it "learns" how to solve them by spotting patterns. Here's how it generally works:

1. **Input Data:** Text, numbers, images, or sound.
2. **Learning:** The AI trains on examples (this is called training).
3. **Model Building:** The system creates a model or pattern.
4. **Prediction or Output:** It gives answers, suggestions, or actions.

It's like teaching a child to recognize animals by showing thousands of pictures.

Real-Life Examples of AI You Already Use

Situation	AI in Action
Watching Netflix	Recommends shows based on your history
Studying online	AI tutors like Khan Academy's "Khanmigo"
Writing essays	ChatGPT helps brainstorm and summarize
Using Google Maps	AI finds the fastest route

Typing on phones	Predictive text, autocorrect
Playing games	Smart NPCs (non-player characters)
Smart assistants	Alexa, Siri, or Google Assistant

Try This – Spot the AI Challenge!

Circle the items that use AI:

1. A microwave oven
2. YouTube recommendations
3. A bicycle
4. ChatGPT
5. Alarm clock with sleep tracker
6. Manual diary
7. Grammarly spell checker
8. Traditional calculator

Answers: 2, 4, 5, 7 (These all use AI!)

AI Around a Student's Day

Here's a glimpse of how AI touches your life from morning to night:

Time	AI-Powered Activity
6:30 AM	Smart alarm adjusts to your sleep cycle
7:00 AM	Music app recommends morning playlist
8:30 AM	School app reminds you of assignments
12:00 PM	Chatbot answers a science doubt
4:00 PM	Grammarly checks homework grammar
6:00 PM	AI tool summarizes history notes
8:00 PM	Reclaim AI helps plan next day's tasks

AI in the Indian Education System

India's NEP 2020 encourages the use of AI in schools to:

- Build digital awareness
- Encourage experiential learning
- Teach critical thinking and real-world problem solving

Schools across India are now integrating AI clubs, coding classes, and productivity tools into everyday learning. The idea is not just to use AI but to understand and build it.

Myths vs. Facts About AI

Myth	Truth
AI is going to replace all humans	AI supports humans; many jobs will change, not vanish
AI can think like a human	AI follows data and logic—not emotions
Only coders can use AI	Anyone can use AI tools with the right guidance
AI is dangerous	When used ethically and safely, AI is helpful

Reflection Corner

- Where have you unknowingly used AI this week?
- Can you name 3 AI tools that help with your learning?
- How do you feel about AI helping with schoolwork—excited or unsure?

Key Takeaways

- AI = Intelligence made by machines. It simulates thinking, learning, and decision-making.

• AI includes tools we use every day—voice assistants, study apps, suggestion engines.
• Machine Learning and Deep Learning are ways through which AI learns from data.
• AI can be narrow (one task) or generative (create text, images, music).
• NEP 2020 promotes the use of AI to prepare students for future-ready skills.

Abeer's Tech Tip
Try asking the same AI question in three different ways. Notice how the answers change. The quality of your prompt changes the quality of your result.
Amaara Asks
If AI learns from human data, can it ever be completely unbiased?

Quick Recap Quiz

Q1. What does AI stand for?
A. Automatic Intelligence
B. Artificial Intelligence
C. Advanced Interface

Q2. Which of these is a Generative AI tool?
A. Midjourney
B. Calculator
C. Keyboard

Q3. Which year did the term AI originate?
A. 1946
B. 1956
C. 1996
Answers: Q1 – B, Q2 – A, Q3 – B

Chapter 2

Why Does AI Matter to Students?

Learning Objectives

By the end of this chapter, you will be able to:
• Recognize how AI impacts your everyday student life.
• Understand the benefits of AI for learning, productivity, and creativity.
• Appreciate why AI literacy is important for personal growth and future careers.
• Understand NEP 2020's emphasis on tech-enabled, competency-based education.
• Reflect on your own digital habits and opportunities to use AI ethically.

So, Why Should You Care About AI?

You might be wondering: "AI sounds cool, but I'm just a student. Why should I care?"
Here's the answer in one line:

AI can help you learn smarter, live better, and prepare for a future full of opportunities.

You already live in a digital world. You use phones, apps, voice assistants, and smart tools every single day. But using technology blindly and understanding technology wisely are very different things.

This chapter will show you why students who understand and use AI responsibly will be better prepared for school, exams, life skills, and even jobs of the future.

AI Is Already a Part of Your Life

Let's take a moment to think about your daily routine. AI is probably involved in:

- Waking you up with a smart alarm.
- Reminding you about a homework deadline.
- Helping you plan a study schedule with Notion AI.
- Suggesting videos on YouTube based on your interests.
- Summarizing class notes using Otter.ai or Tactiq.
- Giving grammar suggestions in your English assignment via Grammarly.
- Creating a project presentation using Canva or Tome AI.

And you didn't even realize that was AI working in the background! AI has become like oxygen in the digital age—it's invisible but vital.

AI Helps You Learn Better and Faster

Here are a few concrete ways AI boosts your learning:

1. Personalized Learning

- AI tools adapt to your pace and level. If you're weak in algebra but strong in science, AI can create a custom study path.

• Platforms like Khan Academy (Khanmigo) or Caktus AI offer chatbot-like tutors.

2. Time Management

• You can organize your day using AI calendars and planners.
• Tools like Reclaim AI and Motion help block distractions and schedule tasks automatically.

3. Note-Taking and Summarizing

• No more scribbling during fast lectures! Tools like Otter.ai and Mindgrasp transcribe and summarize lessons in real time.

4. Memory Boost and Practice

• AI flashcard tools like Quizlet AI help with active recall and spaced repetition, which improves memory retention.

5. Homework Help

• Tools like Socratic and Photomath use AI to explain answers step-by-step, rather than just giving the solution.

Reflection Prompt: Which of these AI tools could have helped you in your last exam preparation?

AI Saves Time and Effort

High school is a juggling act—classes, tuitions, extracurriculars, and now even internships. AI can help you:

• **Automate repetitive tasks:** formatting, grammar checks, copying notes.
• **Organize better:** project planning, reminders, digital filing.
• **Get to the point faster**: summary tools help you read smarter.

Example: Instead of reading 15 pages of a history chapter, you can get the main points summarized in minutes using tools like ChatDOC or Readwise Reader.

It's not about taking shortcuts. It's about using time more efficiently to learn deeper and think better.

AI Aids Personal Growth

AI isn't just about academics. It can help you grow as a person.

Mental Wellness
• AI-powered mood journals and trackers like Wysa or Youper help monitor stress levels.
• Sleep apps with AI adjust alarms based on your sleep patterns.

Building Habits
• AI nudges help you build routines (drink water, take breaks, read daily).
• Tools like SmartKit or Loop Habit Tracker AI use intelligent notifications and reports.

Creative Exploration
• Want to write a song or make a comic strip? AI tools like Suno, Midjourney, or Canva AI unlock new artistic experiences.

Why NEP 2020 Wants You to Learn AI

India's National Education Policy (NEP) 2020 strongly recommends:
• Digital literacy from early school years.
• Exposure to coding, computational thinking, and AI.
• Use of technology to personalize learning.
• Teaching ethical tech usage and critical thinking.

The NEP promotes multidisciplinary learning—that means students of science, commerce, humanities, or arts—all should understand how AI affects their field.

Example:
• A history student may use AI to analyze ancient scripts.
• A commerce student can use AI to predict stock patterns.
• A literature student may use AI to explore writing styles or grammar.

AI is no longer just a computer science subject. It's a life skill.

Case Study: Meet Aarav & Meher – Two Students, Two Paths

Aarav:
• Relies only on textbooks.
• Spends hours typing assignments manually.
• Has no planner, forgets deadlines.
• Gets stressed during exams.

Meher:
• Uses Notion AI to plan weekly tasks.
• Writes essays with the help of ChatGPT drafts, then edits them herself.
• Records lectures on Otter.ai for revision.
• Has a sleep tracker that helps her rest better.

Result? Meher feels more confident, less stressed, and learns smarter—not harder.
You don't have to be a coder like Meher. You just need to be curious, responsible, and open to learning smarter.

AI Today, Career Tomorrow

Today's students will work in jobs that don't even exist yet. But one thing is certain: Almost every career will involve AI.

Here are examples of how students in different streams may use AI:

Stream	AI Use Example
Science	Lab simulations, disease detection models
Commerce	Stock prediction, market analysis
Humanities	Language analysis, historical data tools
Arts & Design	AI-assisted music, graphics, animation
Sports	AI coaching, movement analysis

If you understand AI now, you're future-ready.

But Wait—Is It Okay to Use AI in School?

This is an important question. AI can help, but it should never replace your thinking. Teachers are now encouraging students to use AI ethically, just like you'd use a calculator or dictionary.

Do:
✓ Use AI for idea generation, grammar suggestions, summarizing
✓ Use AI to plan, visualize, and organize work
✓ Learn how the AI tool works

Don't:
× Copy-paste AI essays without understanding
× Use AI to cheat on homework or exams
× Share personal information with unknown AI apps

NEP 2020 also focuses on responsible tech use, which includes:
- Understanding bias and fairness in AI.
- Respecting digital privacy.
- Knowing when to ask for human help.

Quick List: Benefits of AI for Students

Benefit	AI Example Tool
Smart Scheduling	Reclaim AI, SkedPal
Note-Taking & Summaries	Otter.ai, Mindgrasp, Elicit
Learning Support	Khanmigo, Socratic, ChatGPT
Writing Help	Grammarly, Writesonic, Jenni AI
Creative Projects	Canva AI, Tome, Midjourney
Presentation Slides	Gamma, Beautiful.ai, Tome AI
Habit Formation	SmartKit, Habitify AI
Voice Learning	Play.ht, Speechify, ElevenLabs

Try This – Reflect & Write

Take 5 minutes to answer these prompts in your notebook:

1. What's one school-related task you struggle with?
2. Which AI tool could help you do it better?
3. How would you make sure you use that tool ethically?

Key Takeaways

• AI matters to students because it makes learning, organizing, and creating easier and smarter.

• AI helps in personalized education, better time management, and self-improvement.

• NEP 2020 promotes AI awareness to make students future-ready and digitally literate.

• Students must use AI as a companion, not a crutch—supporting their learning, not replacing it.

• The goal is to become ethical, smart, and creative users of technology.

Quick Recap Quiz

Q1. Which of these is NOT a good use of AI in school?
a. Creating a daily planner
b. Using AI to write your exam
c. Summarizing class notes
d. Making creative presentations

Q2. Why does NEP 2020 support AI in education?
a. To replace books
b. To teach only coding
c. To encourage digital literacy and future skills
d. To reduce school time

Q3. What does "ethical use of AI" mean?
a. Hiding that you used AI
b. Using AI with honesty and responsibility
c. Giving personal info to any tool
d. Always agreeing with AI output

Answers: Q1 – B, Q2 – C, Q3 – B

Chapter 3

Where Can You Use AI in Daily Life?

Learning Objectives

By the end of this chapter, you will:

• Understand how AI fits into your daily routine as a student.
• Identify real-life situations where AI can support smart living.
• Explore AI applications in education, home, health, entertainment, and personal productivity.
• Learn how to integrate AI tools into your lifestyle, ethically and effectively.

AI is All Around You—You Just Didn't Notice!

Artificial Intelligence isn't locked away in labs or only accessible to tech experts. In fact, it's quietly helping you every single day—from waking you up in the morning to helping you fall asleep at night. It's time to make AI visible.

Think of AI as your invisible digital assistant—it doesn't have a face, but it helps you stay organized, focused, and informed.

Let's now walk through an AI-powered day in your life and explore where you can apply these tools—at home, in school, during free time, and while preparing for the future.

1. Mornings: Start Smart

✓ How AI helps:

• **Smart Alarms:** Wake you gently at the best moment in your sleep cycle (Sleep Cycle, Alarmy).
• **Daily Summaries:** Apps like Google Assistant or Alexa give you weather, news, and your to-do list.
• **Voice Commands:** Say "Hey Siri, what's my schedule today?"—and you're updated instantly.
• **Habit Trackers**: Apps like Fabulous or Loop remind you to drink water, meditate, or stretch.

Tip: Use an AI-based routine planner to start your day with purpose.

2. In the Classroom: Learn Smarter

Schools are slowly adopting AI, but you don't have to wait. Here's how students use AI tools in school or during self-study:

AI in Note-Taking

• Otter.ai records lectures and creates searchable transcripts.
• Tactiq generates AI summaries of Google Meet or Zoom classes.

AI in Reading & Research

• Elicit simplifies research papers by pulling out key insights.
• ChatDOC scans PDFs and answers questions on the document.

AI as a Learning Assistant

• Socratic by Google explains concepts through step-by-step solutions.
• Khanmigo offers AI-driven tutoring for math and science.
• Caktus AI helps you understand essay prompts and break them down.

Scenario: Struggling to understand a biology concept? Open Khan Academy's AI tutor or ask ChatGPT to explain it in simple language.

3. At Home: Organize, Relax, and Reflect

AI isn't just for learning. It can make your home life smoother and more enjoyable.

Organization and Planning

• Notion AI acts like a digital notebook that organizes your schoolwork, thoughts, and tasks.
• Reclaim AI blocks time for classes, breaks, and assignments on your calendar.
• Motion and SkedPal help you create smart schedules that adjust in real-time.

AI in Entertainment

• Netflix, Spotify, and YouTube use AI to suggest what you might like next.
• Game AIs adjust difficulty levels based on how you play.

Well-being at Home

• Wysa and Youper are AI mental health companions that help you journal and track your mood.
• Smart bulbs and thermostats adjust lighting and temperature automatically.

Try This: Ask your family to try a "smart home day" using AI tools for cooking, alarms, shopping lists, and mood tracking.

4. Studying & Assignments: Boost Productivity

AI is your best study partner—if you use it wisely.

Writing Essays & Assignments
• Grammarly and Jenni AI suggest improvements in sentence structure, tone, and grammar.
• Writesonic or ChatGPT can help generate first drafts or outline ideas.

Research and Summaries
• Scholarcy condenses long papers into short summaries.
• Readwise Reader helps you organize research material from the web.

Smart Revision
• Mindgrasp summarizes video lectures, notes, and YouTube content.
• Recall AI creates practice quizzes based on your material.

Presentations and Visuals
• Canva Magic Design gives you slide templates in seconds.
• Gamma helps you turn an outline into a stunning AI-generated presentation.

Pro Tip: Never submit AI-written content without reviewing and personalizing it. Always bring **your voice** to your work.

5. AI in Family and Community Life

AI tools are not just for individual use. They also help in family routines, community interaction, and group projects.

Family Tasks
• Shared AI calendars help coordinate family schedules.
• Voice assistants like Alexa or Google Home can help plan meals, play music, or manage smart appliances.

Group Work
• Use Notion AI or Google Bard for brainstorming as a group.
• Summarize group meeting notes with Otter.ai.
• Assign project deadlines using ClickUp AI or Trello with AI plugins.

Volunteering & Projects
• Use AI for NGO projects: create posters with Canva AI, or social media posts with Copy.ai.

6. Free Time: Creativity Unleashed

AI can help you create, express, and explore hobbies like never before.

Art & Design
• Midjourney and DALL·E turn words into stunning images.
• Canva AI helps design greeting cards, posters, or logos.

Video and Audio Creation
• Synthesia lets you make videos using AI avatars.
• OpusClip turns long videos into short reels.
• ElevenLabs turns text into realistic voiceovers.

Music and Writing
• Suno AI composes music based on prompts.
• Rytr or Writesonic help you write stories or poems.

Challenge: Create a short comic or music reel using an AI tool and present it in class!

7. Health & Self-Care: AI for Wellness

Taking care of your body and mind is part of being a smart student.
Sleep

• Apps like Sleep Cycle or Pillow use AI to monitor your sleep and wake you gently.

Mental Wellness
• Meditation apps like Headspace or Calm use AI to personalize your sessions.

Fitness
• AI workout apps like Fitbod or Freeletics create routines based on your goals.
• Wearables like Fitbit use AI to track your heart rate and activity.

8. Future Planning: Careers, Skills & Portfolios

Even your dreams need a smart plan. AI can help you:

Plan Your Career
• Use Career AI platforms to explore interests, stream choices, and skill paths.
• Platforms like Unschool AI or Internshala AI tools suggest learning tracks.

Build Your Portfolio
• Document your projects, skills, and achievements on platforms like Notion, Canva Portfolios, or LinkedIn AI resume builders.

Learn New Skills
• Use Google AI courses, Coursera, or Kaggle to build your resume.

Activity: Create your own "Smart Life + Study" dashboard using Notion or Trello with AI plugins.

Reflection Corner: Your AI Touchpoints

Take a few minutes to fill this table with your own experiences:

Area	Current AI Tool I Use	Tool I Want to Try
Study Help		
Notes & Summary		
Time Management		
Wellness & Routine		
Creativity & Projects		

Try This – AI Day Challenge

Spend one full day using at least 5 AI tools:

1. Wake up using a smart alarm.
2. Use a planner to organize your school tasks.
3. Record class notes using an AI note-taker.
4. Use a summary tool to revise a chapter.
5. Create a visual or audio project with AI.

At the end of the day, write one paragraph on: "How did AI make my day better?"

Real-World NEP 2020 Link

This chapter reflects the NEP 2020 goal of:

- Tech-integrated learning.
- Competency-based use of digital tools.
- Personalized, self-directed education.

Students are not just content consumers—they are becoming content creators, organizers, and leaders, powered by ethical AI.

Key Takeaways

- AI can be used throughout the day: in the classroom, at home, while studying, and even during creative time.

• Tools like Notion AI, Canva, Grammarly, and Caktus AI help make your life more productive and enjoyable.
• You don't need to be a tech wizard—just stay curious and explore!
• AI can be your learning buddy, wellness coach, design partner, and career guide—all in one.
• NEP 2020 encourages you to use such tools to become an independent, ethical, and future-ready learner.

Quick Recap Quiz

Q1. Which tool can help summarize your PDF notes?
A. Spotify
B. ChatDOC
C. Camera App
D. Zoom

Q2. Which of these is used for smart scheduling?
A. Paint
B. Motion
C. Compass
D. VLC Player

Q3. What's a creative use of AI mentioned in this chapter?
A. Mug design
B. Comic creation
C. Water boiling
D. Typing in Word

Answers: Q1 – B, Q2 – B, Q3 – B

Chapter 4

Meet Your Digital Helpers

AI Agents & Assistants

Learning Objectives

By the end of this chapter, you will:

• Understand the differences between AI agents, chatbots, and virtual assistants.
• Learn how these digital helpers work behind the scenes.
• Discover examples of active and passive AI agents in your daily life.
• Know how to interact with AI assistants responsibly and effectively.
• Explore real-world use cases for students using these tools.

What Are AI Agents, Chatbots, and Virtual Assistants?

Think of AI agents as digital helpers that act on your behalf. They don't just sit and wait—they observe, learn, and sometimes make decisions for you.

Here's a quick breakdown:

Term	What It Does	Example
AI Agent	Senses the environment, makes decisions, takes action.	Reclaim AI, Smart thermostats
Chatbot	Text-based responder to user questions.	ChatGPT, WhatsApp bots
Virtual Assistant	Interacts through voice or screen to complete tasks.	Siri, Alexa, Google Assistant

What Makes an AI Agent 'Smart'?

AI agents are made of 3 core parts:

1. **Sensors/Input:** Like microphones, cameras, or user commands.
2. **Processing/Logic:** Uses algorithms and data to make decisions.
3. **Action/Output:** Talks, reminds, sends a message, makes a plan.

Example:

When you say, "Remind me to study at 5 PM," your voice assistant hears you, understands the request, and sets a calendar reminder. That's an AI agent at work!

Types of AI Agents in Your Life

There are two main types of AI agents based on how they behave:

1. Passive Agents

- They act only when you command them.
- They don't "think" on their own.

- **Examples:**
    - o Chatbots like ChatGPT.
    - o Siri/Alexa responding to a question.
    - o Customer support bots.

2. Active Agents

- These observe and act without waiting for commands.
- They might alert you, rearrange your schedule, or optimize a system.

- **Examples:**
    - o Reclaim AI reschedules your calendar based on changes.
    - o Smart home systems adjust lighting based on sunset.
    - o Sleep tracker alarm wakes you in your lightest sleep phase.

Tip: Active agents are like assistants who think ahead. Passive agents are like tools you ask to do things.

How Do Chatbots Help in Learning?

Chatbots are simple AI agents that **converse via text.** They are trained to answer questions, assist with tasks, or guide you through a process.

In Education:

- ChatGPT helps generate summaries and ideas.
- Khan Academy's Khanmigo assists in math problems.
- College websites often have bots to answer FAQs on admissions.

In Mental Health:

- Wysa and Youper chatbots offer safe emotional support.
- They help track moods and suggest calming exercises.

In Communication:

- Chatbots on WhatsApp handle bookings, alerts, and even quizzing.
- Telegram bots help with journaling, language learning, etc.

Try This: Ask ChatGPT: "Explain the causes of the French Revolution in 100 words." You'll get a summary instantly.

Meet Your Voice Assistants

Virtual assistants go a step further. They use Natural Language Processing (NLP) to understand spoken language.

Famous examples:
- **Alexa (Amazon)** – Works through smart speakers.
- **Siri (Apple)** – Built into iPhones and iPads.
- **Google Assistant** – Found on Android devices.
- **Bixby (Samsung)** – Offers smart suggestions on Galaxy phones.

What They Can Do for You:
- Set reminders and alarms.
- Play music or podcasts.
- Tell jokes or answer trivia.
- Send texts or make calls.
- Translate languages.
- Find information instantly.

Scenario: Say "Hey Siri, how do you say 'Thank You' in French?" It replies: "Merci."

Smart Tools That Act as Agents

You might already be using these without realizing their intelligence:

Tool	Type	What It Does
Reclaim AI	Active agent	Adjusts your schedule in real-time
Grammarly	Passive assistant	Corrects and suggests improvements as you type

Notion AI	Passive chatbot	Summarizes, rewrites, and answers inside Notion
Alexa Routines	Active agent	Triggers actions like turning on lights, playing news
Sleep Cycle App	Active agent	Sets smart alarms based on your sleep patterns

How Do These Helpers 'Understand' You?

AI agents use a combination of:

- **Natural Language Processing (NLP):** To understand your voice or text.
- **Machine Learning:** To improve over time as they learn your patterns.
- **Data Collection:** Some collect data (like habits or preferences) to customize suggestions.

Reminder:
Always check the privacy settings of AI agents. Not all are 100% safe. Avoid sharing sensitive info.

Comparison Table: Chatbot vs Voice Assistant vs AI Agent

Feature	Chatbot	Voice Assistant	AI Agent
Interface	Text	Voice/Text	Text/Voice + Automation
Initiation	User asks	User speaks	Sometimes auto-initiated
Example Tool	ChatGPT, Khanmigo	Siri, Alexa	Reclaim AI, Smart home

Memory & Learning	Basic	Medium	Advanced personalization
Contextual Decisions	No	Some	Yes

Use Cases for Students

Here are some everyday examples of how digital helpers can boost your life:

Scenario	AI Helper Used
"Wake me up at 6 AM on Monday."	Siri or Google Assistant
"Remind me to revise biology."	Alexa Reminder or Notion AI
"Help me brainstorm essay ideas."	ChatGPT, Writesonic
"Summarize this PDF chapter."	ChatDOC, Mindgrasp, Elicit
"Create a study schedule."	Reclaim AI, StudyMonkey
"Turn on the light when it's dark."	Alexa Smart Home or Google Home

Activity: Make a list of 3 things you do daily that could be handled better by an AI assistant.

Cool Real-World Applications of AI Agents

- Self-driving cars are controlled by powerful AI agents.
- Email sorters (like Gmail's categories) act as passive AI agents.
- Smart fridges monitor what's inside and suggest recipes.
- AI assistants for the visually impaired help navigate and identify objects.

Soon, you'll see AI agents used in:
• Traffic lights that adapt to traffic flow.
• Farming tools that adjust watering schedules.
• Classrooms that personalize tests and assignments.

Think & Reflect

Answer the following in your notebook:
1. Have you ever used a virtual assistant? What did you use it for?
2. Which AI helper would you want as part of your daily routine?
3. Do you prefer typing to a chatbot or talking to a voice assistant? Why?

NEP 2020 Alignment Spotlight

This chapter supports the NEP 2020 goal of:
• Promoting AI awareness at the school level.
• Helping students become digitally fluent and responsible.
• Using tech to support self-directed learning and organization.
• Encouraging familiarity with real-world emerging technologies.

Key Takeaways

• AI agents are tools that sense, decide, and act—like real digital assistants.
• Chatbots respond to text queries and support research, writing, and learning.
• Voice assistants make everyday life smoother through spoken interactions.
• Active AI agents help in planning, adjusting, and responding in real time.
• Using these tools smartly helps students learn faster, plan better, and live more efficiently.

Quick Recap Quiz

Q1. Which of these is an AI agent that adjusts your calendar?
A. Otter.ai
B. Reclaim AI
C. Grammarly
D. Netflix

Q2. What is a chatbot used for?
A. Cleaning your room
B. Voice calling
C. Text-based question answering
D. Cooking food

Q3. What's the difference between an active and passive agent?
A. Passive agents act automatically
B. Active agents only work when you ask
C. Active agents sense and act; passive ones wait for commands
D. They are the same thing

Answers: Q1 – B, Q2 – C, Q3 – C

Chapter 5

Studying Made Smarter with AI

Learning Objectives

By the end of this chapter, you will:

• Discover how AI tools can assist in note-taking, planning, revision, and concept understanding.
• Learn about top AI apps used by students to improve academic performance.
• Understand how to integrate AI ethically into your study routine.
• Explore real-world examples and use cases of smart study practices powered by AI.

The Old Way vs. The Smart Way

Picture this:

• You have a pile of textbooks.
• An approaching deadline for a science project.
• Two pending essays.

• And you haven't revised that history chapter either.

Sound familiar?
Now imagine this:
• A study planner tells you what to do and when.
• An AI tool summarizes your chapter in minutes.
• A chatbot helps you understand tough math problems.
• Your notes are auto-recorded and searchable.
• A smart revision quiz appears, tailored just for you.

Welcome to AI-powered studying—where your time and energy are used smarter, not harder.

Why Use AI for Studying?

Here are the main benefits of using AI tools in your academic routine:

Benefit	How AI Helps
Save Time	Instant summaries, flashcards, reminders
Learn at Your Own Pace	Personalized explanations and feedback
Better Organization	Smart planners and schedule blockers
Boost Understanding	Step-by-step problem solving
Enhance Memory	AI-generated quizzes and revision tools

NEP 2020 Goal Matched: Personalized, competency-based, tech-integrated learning.

1. Smarter Note-Taking and Transcription

Gone are the days of messy, incomplete classroom notes. AI tools can record, transcribe, and organize notes for you.

Tools to Try:

- **Otter.ai** – Records your class and creates searchable notes.
- **Tactiq** – Transcribes Google Meet or Zoom classes in real-time.
- **Mindgrasp** – Summarizes lectures and YouTube videos into notes.

Use Case: Anushka records her physics lecture on Otter.ai, reviews the summary at home, and shares highlights with her group project team.

Try This: Record a science explanation from YouTube. Use Mindgrasp to summarize it into bullet points.

2. Study Planning and Time Management

Planning your study schedule is as important as the studying itself. AI tools help you organize your tasks with precision.

Tools to Try:

- **Notion AI** – Build a subject-wise planner with smart reminders.
- **StudyMonkey** – Generates AI-based daily study plans.
- **Reclaim AI** – Automatically adjusts your calendar based on changes.

Example: If your tuition gets rescheduled, Reclaim AI shifts your revision slot accordingly.

Pro Tip: Block at least 90 minutes daily using AI to focus on high-priority tasks.

3. AI-Powered Study Buddies

Think of AI tutors that never sleep and are always ready to help.

Tools to Try:

- **Khan Academy's Khanmigo** – Solves and explains complex math and science concepts.
- **Socratic by Google** – Snap a pic of a question and get detailed solutions.

• **Caktus AI** – Guides you through writing, coding, or planning.

Scenario: You're stuck on a tough algebra equation. Open Socratic, scan the question, and receive an instant step-by-step breakdown.

Activity: Solve a question on Socratic, then try explaining the same solution to a friend.

4. Chapter Summarizers and Explainers

Reading long chapters just before exams? Use AI to extract key points, headings, and summaries.

Tools to Try:
• **ChatDOC** – Upload any PDF and ask it to summarize or explain.
• **Elicit** – Pulls out answers from long research or academic papers.
• **Scholarcy** – Breaks down research papers into digestible summaries.

Tool	Best For	Link
ChatDOC	School textbooks in PDF form	chatdoc.com
Scholarcy	Class reports or articles	scholarcy.com
Elicit	Deeper research in social science	elicit.org

Task: Upload a chapter PDF to ChatDOC and ask: "Summarize in 10 points for revision."

5. Revision Tools: Quizzes, Flashcards & Memory Boosters

Revision gets boring. But AI can make it interactive, personalized, and even fun.
Tools to Try:
• **Recall AI** – Creates quizzes based on your notes.

• **Quizlet AI** – Builds smart flashcards and practice sets.
• **Brainscape** – Uses spaced repetition and progress tracking.

NEP 2020 Focus: Active recall, metacognition, and skill-based learning.

Example: Priya uses Quizlet to revise biology terms before a test—she sets a 15-minute timer and beats her score daily.

Challenge: Create a custom flashcard deck using Quizlet AI for your next unit test.

6. AI for Subject-Specific Help

AI doesn't just help "in general." It can support **specific subjects** too.

Math:
• **Photomath** – Solves equations with steps.
• **Cymath** – Lightweight app for basic to advanced math.

Science:
• **Explainpaper** – Uploads science papers and explains them in plain English.
• **Khanmigo** – AI tutor with science modules.

English:
• **Grammarly** – Corrects grammar and improves vocabulary.
• **Writesonic** – Helps brainstorm essays or rephrase content.

History/Social Science:
• **ChatGPT** – Ask for cause-effect summaries, timelines, or debate prep.
Prompt Idea: "Explain World War 2 causes in bullet points for a 9th grader."

7. Focus and Productivity Boost

Use AI tools to stay focused, reduce distractions, and work with better concentration.

Tools to Try:
• **Motion** – Schedules deep work blocks intelligently.
• **Serene** – Combines focus timers and smart goal setting.
• **Brain.fm** – Uses AI music to improve focus.

Try This: Set a 30-minute Motion focus session before starting homework. Use Brain.fm in the background.

How to Use AI Ethically in Studying

✓ DO:
• Use AI to brainstorm, organize, and explain.
• Personalize summaries in your own words.
• Acknowledge if AI helped in your assignment.

× DON'T:
• Copy-paste AI-written answers blindly.
• Use AI to cheat in online assessments.
• Replace real learning with shortcuts.

Golden Rule: Use AI to enhance your thinking—not to avoid it.

Smart Study System: Step-by-Step AI Workflow

Here's a practical method to integrate AI into your study routine:
1. **Plan your day/week** – Use StudyMonkey or Notion AI.
2. **Record lessons or classes** – Use Otter.ai or Tactiq.
3. **Summarize topics** – ChatDOC, Mindgrasp, or Scholarcy.
4. **Revise interactively** – Quizlet, Recall AI.
5. **Practice writing** – Grammarly, Writesonic, ChatGPT.

6. **Manage focus** – Motion, Serene, Brain.fm.

Pro Tip: Keep a notebook or digital journal to reflect on what you learned—combine human effort with AI power.

Think & Reflect

Take a few minutes to answer:

1. Which AI tool would help you most with your current schoolwork?
2. What part of studying do you find most stressful—and can AI reduce that?
3. How can you ensure you don't misuse AI while studying?

NEP 2020 Alignment Spotlight

This chapter directly supports:

- **Flexible learning paths:** Students can study and revise at their pace using AI.
- **Skill development:** Tools encourage thinking, summarizing, and reflecting.
- **Technology integration:** AI becomes part of the learner's ecosystem.
- **Ethical awareness:** Understanding limits and responsibilities of AI usage.

Key Takeaways

- AI helps students plan, learn, revise, and practice more effectively.
- Tools like Otter.ai, Socratic, Notion AI, Quizlet, and ChatGPT make study time smarter.
- Use subject-specific AI tools for focused help in math, science, history, or writing.
- Combining AI tools with discipline and ethics gives you a real learning edge.
- NEP 2020 encourages these smart, tech-powered learning approaches.

Abeer's Tech Tip
Before using AI to summarize a chapter, read it once yourself. Then compare your understanding with the AI summary.
Amaara Asks
Does faster learning always mean deeper learning?

Quick Recap Quiz

Q1. Which tool can help you create flashcards for revision?
A. Otter.ai
B. Quizlet
C. Motion
D. Grammarly

Q2. What is StudyMonkey used for?
A. Watching videos
B. Writing essays
C. Making study schedules
D. Listening to music

Q3. Why is it wrong to submit AI-written content as your own?
A. It's allowed in all schools
B. It helps you pass quickly
C. It's plagiarism and stops your own learning
D. It earns bonus marks

Answers: Q1 – B, Q2 – C, Q3 – C

Chapter 6

Writing, Reading & Research with AI

Learning Objectives

By the end of this chapter, you will:
• Discover AI tools that enhance writing, editing, summarizing, and paraphrasing.
• Learn how AI can assist in reading comprehension and text analysis.
• Explore responsible use of AI for writing and research purposes.
• Build skills in organizing information, citing sources, and improving clarity using AI support.

The Power of Words in a Digital World

Writing and reading are core skills for every student, no matter your stream. Whether you're working on an essay, writing an answer in an exam, or reading a long passage, communication is key. But it's not always easy.

What if AI could help?
Imagine writing an essay in half the time with grammar checks, creative suggestions, and formatting help. Or summarizing a 12-page history article into clear points. Or rephrasing complex sentences for clarity. That's where AI steps in—not to write for you, but to write with you.

1. AI for Writing Assistance

AI can help you plan, write, edit, and polish your assignments, essays, reports, and creative work.

Tools You Can Use:
- **Grammarly** – Checks spelling, grammar, clarity, and tone.
- **ChatGPT** – Helps brainstorm, outline, rephrase, or complete writing.
- **Jenni AI** – Assists with academic writing using citations.
- **Writesonic** – Generates blog-style, essay-like drafts.
- **Quillbot** – Paraphrases and simplifies text.

Task	AI Tool Suggestion
Fix grammar	Grammarly, Ginger AI
Paraphrase	Quillbot, ChatGPT
Outline structure	Writesonic, Jenni AI
Vocabulary improvement	Grammarly
Sentence rewriter	Wordtune, Grammarly

Use Case: Essay Help

Topic: "The Importance of Clean Energy"

Step 1: Ask ChatGPT: "Give me a 5-point outline on clean energy."

Step 2: Use Writesonic to expand each point into a paragraph.

Step 3: Paste the result into Grammarly to fix language.

Step 4: Use Quillbot to paraphrase or simplify complex lines.

NEP 2020 Alignment: Competency-based writing support, digital fluency, and clarity of communication.

2. AI in Reading and Comprehension

AI can help you understand long or complex texts faster and more clearly.

Whether you're reading an academic article or a dense chapter, AI can summarize, highlight key points, and simplify vocabulary.

Tools You Can Use:
- ChatDOC – Upload PDFs and ask questions directly.
- PDFgear AI – Read and annotate documents using AI summaries.
- Readwise Reader – Helps organize, highlight, and annotate articles.
- Scholarcy – Breaks down research into summaries and flashcards.

Tool	Best For
ChatDOC	Asking questions from PDFs
PDFgear AI	Reading support with notes
Scholarcy	Academic journal summaries
Readwise	Highlighting and organizing

Try This: Upload a history chapter PDF into ChatDOC and ask: "What are the 3 main causes of the Revolt of 1857?"

3. Paraphrasing and Rewriting

Paraphrasing means writing the same idea in a new way. AI helps students avoid plagiarism and improve clarity.

How It Helps:
- Makes your writing more original.
- Explains ideas in simpler words.
- Helps when you're stuck rewriting a tough paragraph.

Tools You Can Use:
- Quillbot – Offers standard, formal, and creative paraphrasing.
- Wordtune – Suggests different sentence versions.
- ChatGPT – Rewrites with tone control.

Example:
Original: "Climate change is a pressing global concern."
Paraphrased: "The world is facing a serious challenge due to climate change."

Tip: Don't just rely on AI—read the result, and make sure it sounds like you.

4. Citation and Referencing

AI writing assistants like Jenni AI or Research Rabbit help you find credible sources and build citations in MLA, APA, or Chicago style.

Why It Matters: Plagiarism is a serious issue. Citing your sources is both ethical and professional.

Tools You Can Use:
- **Jenni AI** – Citation-aware academic writing.
- **Zotero** – AI-assisted bibliography manager.
- **CiteThisForMe** – Auto-generates citation formats.

Activity: Pick any article from the web and create MLA, APA, and Chicago citations using an AI citation generator.

5. Improving Creative Writing

AI doesn't only work for formal assignments—it can help you get creative too.

Examples:

• Writing a poem using a theme (e.g., nature).
• Creating character descriptions for a story.
• Brainstorming titles, dialogue, or metaphors.

Tools You Can Use:

• **Rytr** – Creative writing generator.
• **Sudowrite** – Story continuation and tone enhancer.
• **ChatGPT** – Generate plots, opening lines, or poems.

Fun Prompt: "Write a haiku about exams using AI."

6. Researching with AI: Smarter, Faster, Deeper

Research is more than Googling. AI helps you go deeper—finding scholarly papers, summarizing findings, and answering questions with evidence.

Tools You Can Use:

• **Elicit** – Helps you search academic papers and answer research questions.
• **Consensus** – Finds science-backed answers with citations.
• **Research Rabbit** – Visualizes research connections.
• **Semantic Scholar** – Finds trusted, peer-reviewed papers.

Example: Ask Elicit: "What are the effects of social media on teenage sleep?"
It shows you multiple research papers with key takeaways.

Bonus Tip: Use these tools for project work, debate prep, or extended essays.

AI Writing Workflow: Step-by-Step

1. **Research** using Elicit or Scholarcy.
2. **Outline** your structure with ChatGPT or Writesonic.
3. **Draft** your content and expand ideas using Rytr or Jenni AI.
4. **Review Grammar** using Grammarly or Ginger.
5. **Paraphrase & Polish** with Quillbot or Wordtune.
6. **Check citations** using CiteThisForMe or Zotero.

NEP 2020 Skill Applied: Multimodal literacy and digital writing proficiency.

Use AI in Writing Responsibly

✓ DO:

- Use AI for feedback and support.
- Rewrite outputs in your own words.
- Cite sources correctly.
- Ask for grammar or clarity suggestions.

✗ DON'T:

- Copy-paste AI essays as your own.
- Use AI during exams or take-home tests.
- Trust AI blindly—always double-check facts.
- Share sensitive data with random AI apps.

Golden Rule: Let AI help you think, not think for you.

Real-Life Scenarios

Scenario	AI Tool Support
Essay writing stuck	Use ChatGPT for outline ideas
Grammar weak in English	Use Grammarly to fix issues

Need to simplify a science paragraph	Use Quillbot or ChatGPT
Research for history project	Use Elicit and Consensus
Organize citations for a report	Use Jenni AI or Zotero

Student Voices

"Before AI, I'd spend hours fixing grammar. Now, Grammarly helps me finish drafts faster." – **Samar, Class 11**

"ChatGPT helps me brainstorm debate points, but I always write the final version myself." – **Pallavi, Class 10**

"Elicit made my biology project easier. I found 3 research papers in 10 minutes!" – **Vikas, Class 12**

Think & Reflect

- Have you ever used AI for writing? How?
- What writing task do you struggle with the most?
- How can AI make you a more confident and independent writer?

NEP 2020 Alignment Spotlight

This chapter reflects:

- Focus on digital writing fluency and tool-based learning.
- Encouragement of project-based research and analysis.
- Support for personalized learning environments.
- Emphasis on ethical technology use and critical thinking.

Key Takeaways

- AI supports better writing, reading, and researching for students.
- Tools like Grammarly, ChatGPT, Elicit, and Quillbot improve

clarity, structure, and understanding.

• You still need to bring your voice, judgment, and ethics into the writing process.

• With the right use of AI, your schoolwork becomes more efficient, engaging, and impactful.

Quick Recap Quiz

Q1. Which tool helps you check grammar and clarity?
A. Rytr
B. Grammarly
C. Elicit
D. Sleep Cycle

Q2. Which of these can simplify a PDF document?
A. ChatGPT
B. PDFgear AI
C. Spotify
D. Motion

Q3. What is the golden rule of using AI in writing?
A. Use AI for everything
B. Use AI to think for you
C. Let AI support your thinking, not replace it
D. Always copy-paste AI content

Answers: Q1 – B, Q2 – B, Q3 – C

Chapter 7

AI for Smarter Scheduling & Time Management

Learning Objectives

By the end of this chapter, you will:

- Understand the importance of time management for students.
- Learn how AI tools can help schedule tasks, block distractions, and automate routines.
- Discover top AI-based apps for planning and focus.
- Build a personal time management system using smart digital assistants.
- Reflect on how balanced routines support better learning and mental health.

Why Time Management Is Your Superpower

Every student gets the same 24 hours a day. But why do some manage to:

- Finish their homework,

• Practice a hobby,
• Exercise,
• Sleep well,
• And still feel relaxed…

…while others struggle with deadlines, feel rushed, and miss out?

The answer is not just discipline—it's smart time management.

Now, with AI on your side, managing time doesn't have to feel like a battle. You can build a personalized schedule that adjusts as life changes, reminds you when to focus or rest, and nudges you toward your goals—without needing a human tutor.

What Makes AI Perfect for Scheduling?

AI is good at:
• Understanding your routines,
• Noticing when your plans change,
• Predicting how much time tasks take,
• Helping you stay on track.

Unlike traditional to-do lists, AI scheduling apps can learn your behavior, optimize time blocks, and auto-reschedule when needed.

Let's explore how.

1. Creating the Perfect Study Calendar

A good study calendar:
• Has clear goals,
• Includes breaks,
• Balances school, rest, and free time,
• Adapts to unexpected changes.

Tools You Can Use:

- **Reclaim AI** – Syncs with your Google Calendar and auto-schedules your priorities.
- **Motion** – Combines calendar, to-do list, and focus manager.
- **SkedPal** – Reschedules tasks based on urgency and availability.

Feature	Reclaim AI	Motion	SkedPal
Calendar integration	✓	✓	✓
Auto time blocking	✓	✓	✓
Rescheduling missed tasks	✓	✓	✓
Focus timer	×	✓	✓
Ease of use for students	High	Medium	Medium

Example: You have an exam in 3 days and a dance practice. Reclaim AI finds time gaps, blocks revision time, and reschedules your less urgent tasks.

2. Breaking Big Tasks into Smart Chunks

AI can help you split assignments and goals into small, trackable pieces.

Try this:

- Use Notion AI or Todoist with AI to create a study checklist.

- **Break your project into:**
    - o Research
    - o Planning
    - o Drafting
    - o Editing
    - o Submitting

Activity: Pick your next assignment. Ask ChatGPT:
"Break this task into 5 mini-deadlines over 3 days."

3. Beating Procrastination with Smart Nudges

Let's be honest—sometimes we just don't feel like it. But AI tools can help by:

- Sending intelligent reminders,
- Nudging you at ideal times,
- Blocking distractions during focus sessions.

Tools You Can Use:

- **Serene** – Combines planning and deep focus timers.
- **Forest App** – Grow a tree while staying off your phone.
- **RescueTime** – Monitors app usage and warns you when you're distracted.
- **Clockwise** – Creates "focus time" in your schedule automatically.

Try This:

Use Forest for a 30-minute study sprint. Every time you leave the app, your virtual tree dies. Gamified discipline!

4. Building a Balanced Daily Routine with AI

An effective routine includes:

- Study time
- Breaks
- Meals
- Exercise
- Sleep
- Hobbies

AI planners like Bento, Reclaim, or Motion allow you to:

- Set recurring habits (daily walk, meditation, reading).
- Mix work and wellness.

• Use insights to improve your rhythm.

Time Slot	Task	Tool Used
6:30 AM	Wake up (smart alarm)	Sleep Cycle
7:00 AM	Review tasks	Reclaim AI
9:00 AM–12 PM	School or study	Motion Scheduler
1:00 PM	Break & walk	Forest / Bento
4:00 PM	Homework session	Notion AI
6:00 PM	Hobbies or revision	SkedPal
10:00 PM	Sleep tracker on	Sleep Cycle App

5. Smart Planning for Exams and Projects

When exams are around the corner, planning matters even more.

Step-by-step with AI:

1. List your subjects and exam dates.
2. Use ChatGPT or Caktus AI to plan revision chapters per day.
3. Feed that schedule into Motion or Reclaim.
4. Use a focus timer app to avoid burnout.
5. Review summaries with Mindgrasp or Elicit.

Tip: Tell ChatGPT:
"I have 5 days. Help me plan a study timetable for Class 10 Maths."

6. Managing Stress and Burnout with AI

Good time management = less stress = better results.

AI Tools That Help:

• **Sleep Cycle** – Adjusts alarm based on sleep phases.
• **Headspace** – AI-led meditation sessions.

• **Wysa AI** – Emotional support chatbot.
• **Daily Planner AI** – Sends encouraging quotes, affirmations.

Real Student Experience:
"I felt overwhelmed. Reclaim AI broke my week into clear tasks, and Headspace helped me stay calm." – Simran, Class 11

7. AI Assistants for Multi-Tasking and Reminders

Sometimes you just need a reminder or a digital brain.

Use voice assistants like:
• "Hey Siri, remind me to revise science at 7 PM."
• "Alexa, add 'submit assignment' to my task list."

Combine with:
• Notion AI – For task tracking
• Google Keep + Bard AI – Smart lists and suggestions

Watch Out: Don't Over-Automate

AI should assist, not control.

• If your AI reschedules your study time but you ignore it—you're still responsible.
• Don't let planners turn into stress triggers. Keep them flexible.
• Allow room for human judgment. Plans should guide, not boss you around.

Build Your AI-Enhanced Time Plan (Mini-Project)

Create your own Weekly Smart Planner:
1. Choose a planner tool: Reclaim, Notion, or Motion.
2. List 3 subjects, 2 hobbies, and 1 goal.
3. Set reminders, focus sessions, and rest blocks.

4. Reflect on your progress by the weekend.

Bonus: Share your AI-generated plan with your teacher or parent. Show how you're owning your time.

NEP 2020 Alignment Spotlight

This chapter reflects:
• Life skills development through time planning.
• Self-directed learning using smart technology.
• Digital wellbeing and healthy routines.
• 21st-century skill building—organization, reflection, productivity.

Key Takeaways

• AI scheduling tools help organize your life, reduce stress, and boost results.
• Tools like Reclaim AI, Motion, Forest, and Notion AI make time planning simple and dynamic.
• Balanced schedules include study, rest, health, and hobbies.
• You're in charge—AI assists you but you decide what matters.

Quick Recap Quiz

Q1. Which AI tool reschedules your calendar based on priorities?
A. Grammarly
B. Reclaim AI
C. ChatGPT
D. Spotify

Q2. What is Forest App used for?
A. Studying biology
B. Playing games
C. Tracking how long you focus
D. Planting real trees

Q3. What is the main benefit of Motion App?

A. Music suggestions

B. Auto-organizing your to-dos into a calendar

C. Homework grading

D. Weather updates

Answers: Q1 – B, Q2 – C, Q3 – B

Chapter 8

Creativity Unleashed

AI in Art, Design & Presentations

Learning Objectives

By the end of this chapter, you will:

- Discover how AI is used in creative fields like design, art, video, and presentations.
- Learn about powerful AI tools that support students in creative projects.
- Understand how to balance creativity and automation with ethical use.
- Explore practical school applications: posters, slides, videos, comics, and branding.
- Build confidence in expressing your ideas using digital tools.

Creativity in the Age of AI

Creativity isn't limited to pencils and paintbrushes anymore.

Today, with just a few clicks, AI can help you:

- Generate art,

• Create music,
• Build slide decks,
• Design logos,
• Make comics and videos,
• Write stories or scripts.

AI tools are your co-creators—they follow your ideas, offer new suggestions, and help bring visions to life, even if you don't know how to draw or code.

NEP 2020 Focus: Encourage creative expression using technology and integrate arts with academic learning.

1. AI in Visual Design and Art

Let's start with AI image generators. These tools turn words into pictures using prompts.

Tools to Try:
• **Canva AI (Magic Design)** – Create posters, flyers, cards, resumes.
• **DALL·E 3 (via ChatGPT)** – Generates detailed artwork from text prompts.
• **Midjourney** – Advanced visual art generator (used by professionals).
• **Craiyon** – Simple cartoon image maker for beginners.
• **Fotor AI** – Edits and enhances images intelligently.

Prompt Example: "A classroom on the moon with children learning math using floating tablets – cartoon style."

Use Cases for Students:
• Art projects and visual storytelling.
• Making school event posters.
• Designing creative resumes or digital portfolios.
• Visual aids for history or science models.

Try This: Use Canva AI to design a campaign poster for "Say No to Plastic." Then, create an alternate version using DALL·E.

2. AI for School Presentations and Slide Decks

Do you dread making presentations? AI tools now do the design and writing for you!

Tools to Try:
- **Tome AI** – Creates full presentations with images, titles, content, and design in one click.
- **Gamma App** – Builds elegant slides from outlines or prompts.
- **Canva AI Presentations** – Easy drag-and-drop tool with AI writing help.

Feature	Tome AI	Gamma	Canva AI
Content generation	✓	✓	✓
Design suggestions	✓	✓	✓
AI image creation	✓	×	✓
Collaboration features	Limited	Yes	Yes
Ease for students	High	High	High

Example: You type "My Solar System Project" into Tome, and it generates a 6-slide deck with facts, visuals, and transitions.

Activity: Choose a science topic. Create one slide manually and another with Gamma. Compare both.

3. AI for Posters, Logos, and Infographics

Posters are used in:
- School competitions,
- Awareness campaigns,

• Science fairs,
• Project charts.

Tools to Try:
• **Canva AI** – Create posters from pre-built templates with smart suggestions.
• **Designs.ai** – Build brand kits, logos, and infographics.
• **Visme AI** – Infographics and reports with drag-and-drop features.

Project Idea: Create a "Say No to Cyberbullying" poster using Canva. Add an infographic on online safety using Visme.

4. AI for Video Creation and Editing

Videos are powerful tools for school projects, YouTube channels, and awareness campaigns. AI helps you create, edit, and stylize them without needing a film crew!

Tools to Try:
• **Synthesia** – Make videos using talking AI avatars (great for explainer videos).
• **Lumen5** – Turn blog posts or scripts into animated videos.
• **OpusClip** – Turn long videos into short social clips with subtitles.
• **Runway ML** – Advanced video editing with AI effects.
• **Pictory AI** – Converts text into narration-based videos.

Use Cases:
• Creating project presentations or experiment explainers.
• Making campaign videos for school clubs or events.
• Editing interview videos for social media.

Activity: Record a short message on environmental awareness. Use Pictory AI to turn it into a narrated video.

5. AI for Comics, Storyboards, and Narratives

Love comics or storytelling?

AI can help you:

- Write scripts,
- Generate characters,
- Create comic panels.

Tools to Try:

- **StoryboardThat** – Drag-and-drop comic builder.
- **Pixton** – Custom comic characters for schools.
- **ToonyTool** – Cartoon maker with speech bubbles.
- **ChatGPT + Midjourney** – Create story + visuals together.

Prompt: "A superhero girl from India who solves climate problems with her AI-powered drone."

Project Idea: Turn this into a 6-panel comic using StoryboardThat.

6. AI for Music, Sound, and Voiceovers

Whether you're making a podcast, project video, or just experimenting—AI makes music and sound creation easy.

Tools to Try:

- **Soundraw or Beatoven** – Generate background music.
- **Suno AI** – AI music with lyrics and melody.
- **ElevenLabs** – AI-generated voiceovers in multiple languages.
- **Play.ht** – Turn text into realistic audio.

Example: You write a poem on peace. Use Suno to turn it into a song. Use ElevenLabs for the voiceover.

Try This: Turn your next poetry assignment into a musical rendition using AI.

7. Enhancing Creativity Through Collaboration

Don't just use AI for fun—use it to collaborate with peers on creative schoolwork.

Ideas:

- Group project presentations with AI-designed slides.
- Art exhibitions with AI-generated visuals + hand-drawn elements.
- History timelines built as comics.
- English projects combining storytelling and visual art.
- Student newsletters designed using Canva AI + ChatGPT.

Bonus Tip: Use Notion AI to organize group ideas, track progress, and assign creative tasks.

Use AI Creatively—But Ethically

✓ DO:

- Use AI to support your ideas.
- Credit AI tools when used in group projects.
- Mix AI with original effort (drawings, writing, narration).
- Explore diverse tools to find your creative style.

× DON'T:

- Submit AI-generated art as original in competitions.
- Use offensive or plagiarized content.
- Ignore copyright or school guidelines.

Golden Rule: AI can amplify your creativity—but it cannot replace your unique imagination.

Creative AI Toolkit for Students

Tool Name	Best For	Free Version	Link
Canva AI	Posters & presentations	✓	https://canva.com
Tome AI	Slide decks	✓	https://tome.app
Gamma	Presentations	✓	https://gamma.app
Midjourney	Artistic image creation	×	https://midjourney.com
DALL·E	Illustrations from prompts	✓ (via ChatGPT)	https://openai.com/dall-e
StoryboardThat	Comics & storyboards	✓	https://storyboardthat.com
Synthesia	Video creation with avatars	×	https://synthesia.io
Suno AI	AI-generated music	✓	https://suno.com
ElevenLabs	Voiceovers	✓ (limited)	https://elevenlabs.io

Think & Reflect

- What is one school project where you can use AI for design or storytelling?
- How can you combine your personal creativity with AI tools?
- What does "creative responsibility" mean when using AI?

NEP 2020 Alignment Spotlight

This chapter supports:
• Multidisciplinary learning through tech + arts integration.
• Building 21st-century skills like creativity, collaboration, and communication.
• Using digital tools to enhance expression and project-based learning.
• Ethical awareness while using AI-generated content.

Key Takeaways

• AI tools empower students to design, write, and create like never before.
• Platforms like Canva, Tome, Midjourney, Synthesia, and Suno offer easy access to professional-level outputs.
• Combine AI with human emotion, originality, and ethics for the best results.
• Every student—artist or not—can now express their ideas visually,

Abeer's Tech Tip
Use AI-generated design as a base layer — then customize colors, text, and structure yourself.
Amaara Asks
If AI creates art, who owns creativity?

Quick Recap Quiz

Q1. Which tool helps create entire slide decks from a single topic prompt?
A. Canva
B. ChatGPT
C. Tome AI
D. Forest App

Q2. Which AI tool generates realistic voices from text?

A. Soundraw

B. OpusClip

C. ElevenLabs

D. Pixton

Q3. What's a safe practice when using AI in competitions?

A. Submit without changes

B. Hide AI usage

C. Combine with original work and give credit

D. Use AI only for marks

Answers: Q1 – C, Q2 – C, Q3 – C

Chapter 9

Talking, Listening & Understanding Better with AI

Learning Objectives

By the end of this chapter, you will:

- Understand how AI enhances communication through voice, text, and translation.
- Explore tools that improve listening, speaking, and language skills.
- Learn how AI supports special needs and inclusive education.
- Discover real-world uses of speech-to-text, voice assistants, and AI language learners.
- Practice communicating better with AI companions.

Communication is More Than Talking

In school and in life, how you communicate shapes how others understand you—and how you understand the world. Good communication isn't just about speaking clearly. **It's also about:**

• Listening well,
• Reading with understanding,
• Asking questions,
• Explaining your thoughts confidently,
• Using different languages when needed.

What if AI could help you improve all of that?
Today's AI tools can listen to you, speak with you, translate for you, and explain difficult concepts in simpler words—instantly. It's like having a personal tutor, translator, and companion in your pocket.

1. Voice Assistants – Smart Conversations Made Easy

We already met Siri, Alexa, and Google Assistant earlier. These voice assistants are more than just question-answer bots—they help you think aloud, stay organized, and learn by speaking.

Use Cases for Students:
• Ask questions aloud: "Hey Google, who discovered gravity?"
• Set voice reminders: "Alexa, remind me to submit my homework."
• Translate words instantly: "Hey Siri, how do I say 'good luck' in Spanish?"
• Check spellings and meanings.
• Practice English pronunciation.

Tip: Use voice commands during your commute, while cooking, or during breaks to make learning conversational.

2. Voice-to-Text – Turn Your Thoughts into Words

Sometimes we think faster than we can type. AI tools help by converting your voice into text with amazing accuracy.

Tools You Can Use:
• **Otter.ai** – Live transcriptions of meetings or lectures.

• **SpeechTexter** – Speak to write essays, notes, or emails.
• **Google Docs Voice Typing** – Dictate directly in your document.
• **Notta AI** – Converts recordings into editable transcripts.

Use Case: Aarav brainstorms his essay idea while walking. He uses SpeechTexter to record his voice and later edits the text into paragraphs.

Try This: Speak out a diary entry or poem using Google Docs' voice typing. Then format and edit it into final form.

3. Text-to-Speech – Listening to Learn

Do you prefer listening over reading? AI tools can read aloud articles, notes, and books, making learning more engaging.

Tools to Try:
• **Play.ht** – Converts text into realistic human voices.
• **Speechify** – Reads out PDFs, docs, and articles.
• **Natural Readers** – Web-based tool for reading any uploaded content.
• **ElevenLabs** – High-quality multilingual narration voices.

Benefits:
• Learn while resting your eyes.
• Revise by listening to notes.
• Improve pronunciation by hearing new words.
• Helps students with dyslexia or reading difficulties.

NEP 2020 Link: Supports inclusive and personalized learning pathways.

4. Language Learning with AI

Want to learn French, improve your English, or explore Japanese anime in original subtitles? AI tools can make that journey easier and more fun.

Tools to Try:
• **Duolingo** – Fun gamified app for learning over 30+ languages.
• **Google Translate + Camera** – Translate signs or pages instantly.
• **DeepL Translator** – Known for more accurate translations than Google.
• **ChatGPT** – Ask for grammar explanations, sentence corrections, or conversational phrases.

Prompt Idea: Ask ChatGPT:
"How do I introduce myself in French? Explain with pronunciation tips."

5. AI for Accessibility & Inclusive Learning

AI makes communication more inclusive for students who are:
• Visually impaired,
• Hearing impaired,
• Neurodivergent (like dyslexia or ADHD),
• Learning in non-native languages.

Assistive AI Examples:
• **Seeing AI (by Microsoft)** – Describes surroundings for visually impaired users.
• **AVA** – Real-time captions for hearing-impaired students.
• **Otter.ai** – Helps deaf students follow classroom discussions.
• **Speechify & Immersive Reader** – Helps with reading challenges.

Real Story:
Radhika, a student with dyslexia, uses Immersive Reader to have her textbook read aloud at a slow pace with syllable highlighting. She's now more confident in reading aloud.

6. Conversational Practice & Confidence Building

Want to improve spoken English or prepare for an oral presentation? AI can help!

Tools You Can Use:

• **Elsa Speak** – Practice English pronunciation with instant feedback.
• **YouGlish** – Hear how words are used in real sentences.
• **HelloTalk** – Chat with native speakers in different languages.
• **ChatGPT** Voice Mode – Practice conversations on any topic.

Practice Prompt:
"ChatGPT, pretend you're my interview coach. Ask me 3 questions for a school debate tryout."

Bonus Tip: Record yourself using AI-generated interview or speech questions. Then review and improve.

7. Enhancing Understanding in Any Subject

Sometimes we don't need to speak—but we still need help in understanding what we're reading or listening to.

AI can:

• Summarize long chapters (ChatGPT, Mindgrasp).
• Translate scientific words into simple terms (Explainpaper).
• Break down audio lectures into digestible notes (Otter.ai).
• Help you pronounce and define difficult terms (Merriam-Webster + audio).

Prompt Example:
"Explain the greenhouse effect to a 9th grader using an analogy."

Outcome: ChatGPT might say,
"It's like a blanket around the Earth that keeps it warm. But too much blanket causes overheating."

8. From Shy to Confident – How AI Helps in Speaking Practice

Speaking in class or public can feel scary. But AI tools provide a safe, non-judgmental space to practice.

Benefits:
- Try as many times as you want.
- No fear of being laughed at.
- Build confidence before speaking to real people.
- Record, review, improve.

Activity: Write a 2-minute speech on a topic you love. Practice reading it aloud using an AI speech app. Add background music using Soundraw for fun!

Student-Friendly AI Toolkit for Communication

Tool Name	Purpose	Free Version	Platform
Otter.ai	Live transcription & summary	✓	Web, App
Speechify	Text-to-speech reading	✓ (limited)	Web, iOS, Android
Play.ht	Voiceover & narration	✓	Web
ChatGPT	Voice/text conversations	✓	Web, App
Duolingo	Language learning	✓	App
DeepL	High-accuracy translation	✓	Web, Extension
ELSA Speak	English pronunciiation coaching	✓ (limited)	App

Seeing AI	Accessibility tool for vision	✓	iOS

NEP 2020 Alignment Spotlight

This chapter supports:
• Multilingualism and linguistic skills.
• Personalized and inclusive learning.
• Use of technology for enhanced comprehension.
• Bridging language gaps in education.

Key Takeaways

• AI makes communication easier, clearer, and more inclusive.
• From voice assistants to reading tools, students can speak, listen, and understand better with AI.
• These tools boost language learning, pronunciation, public speaking, and confidence.
• Ethical, regular use of these tools leads to smarter communication in academics and life.

Quick Recap Quiz

Q1. Which AI tool converts your speech into written notes?
A. Canva
B. Otter.ai
C. Grammarly
D. Duolingo

Q2. What is DeepL used for?
A. Mind reading
B. Grammar checks
C. Translations
D. Video editing

Q3. How does AI support students with reading challenges?

A. Makes text harder

B. Reads aloud content with highlights

C. Blocks reading apps

D. Erases difficult words

Answers: Q1 – B, Q2 – C, Q3 – B

Chapter 10

Health, Wellness, and AI Life Hacks

Learning Objectives

By the end of this chapter, you will:
• Understand how AI supports physical and mental well-being.
• Explore AI tools for sleep tracking, stress relief, fitness, and healthy routines.
• Learn smart life hacks using AI to build better habits.
• Reflect on how wellness affects academic success and personal growth.
• Create your own balanced AI-powered wellness plan.

Why Health and Wellness Matter for Students

Being productive or smart doesn't just depend on how many hours you study or how fast you use AI tools.

It also depends on:
• How well you sleep,

• How active your body is,
• How balanced your diet is,
• How calm and happy your mind feels.

Wellness = Academic Success + Emotional Strength + Physical Energy
NEP 2020 promotes "holistic development", which includes physical education, mental health awareness, and habit formation—all areas where AI can be your secret support system.

1. Sleep Smarter with AI

Teenagers need 8–10 hours of sleep, but most students don't get enough because of:
• Late-night phone use,
• Stress or anxiety,
• Lack of routine.

AI can help by:
• Tracking your sleep patterns,
• Waking you up at the right time,
• Suggesting ways to improve rest.

Tools to Try:
• **Sleep Cycle** – Smart alarm based on your lightest sleep phase.
• **Pillow** – Tracks sleep stages and suggests improvements.
• **SleepScore** – Gives a daily sleep score and coaching tips.
• **Fitbit/Smartwatch AI** – Monitors sleep with body movements.

Activity: Use a sleep tracker for one week. Reflect: Do you feel more rested on days with longer deep sleep?

2. Mindfulness, Focus & Mental Calm

With exams, peer pressure, screen time, and social media—it's easy to feel mentally tired.

AI tools can help you:
• Practice breathing and meditation,
• Track moods,
• Talk to an AI mental wellness coach,
• Receive positive affirmations.

Tools to Try:
• **Headspace** – AI-curated meditation sessions and sleep sounds.
• **Wysa** – Mental wellness chatbot for stress, anxiety, and emotions.
• **Youper** – AI emotional coach with daily check-ins.
• **MindDoc** – Tracks mood and offers cognitive tips.

Try This: Use Headspace before bed for 5 days. See if your sleep and focus improve.

3. AI-Powered Fitness Motivation

Physical activity helps your brain perform better. But how do you stay consistent?

AI fitness apps guide your:
• Daily workouts,
• Posture correction,
• Step goals,
• Activity plans based on mood or schedule.

Tools to Try:
• **Fitbod** – Creates gym/home workouts based on your goals.
• **Nike Training Club** – Uses AI to suggest workouts.
• **Seven** – 7 Minute Workouts – AI-generated quick sessions.
• **Freeletics AI Coach** – Adjusts your plan as you improve.
Pro Tip: Use Fitbit or Google Fit to set a daily step target (start with 5000).

4. Smart Eating with AI Nutrition Assistants

What you eat directly affects your energy, focus, and mood.

AI tools can:
• Recommend healthy meals,
• Track your calorie and nutrient intake,
• Suggest hydration reminders,
• Help manage emotional eating.

Tools to Try:
• **MyFitnessPal** – Tracks food and calories.
• **YAZIO AI** – Suggests personalized meal plans.
• **WaterMinder** – Sends water reminders based on your weight and activity.
• **Lumen AI (advanced)** – Analyzes breath to suggest carb/fat balance.

Activity: Log your meals for 3 days. Ask ChatGPT: "How can I improve my diet as a school-going student in India?"

5. Build Habits That Stick – Using AI Nudges

Habits are small actions done daily. AI can help you:
• Track progress,
• Send reminders,
• Encourage you when you slip,
• Suggest better timing.

Tools to Try:
• **Habitica** – Turns your goals into a game with rewards.
• **Streaks App** – Visualizes your daily progress.
• **Loop Habit Tracker** – Data-based habit building.
• **Fabulous AI Coach** – Daily self-care routines built over weeks.

Challenge: Set a 7-day "No Junk Food" or "Read 10 pages" challenge using any habit app.

6. AI Life Hacks – Productivity + Well-Being

These smart AI-powered tricks can make your daily routine smoother and more mindful.

Life Hacks:
- **AI Journaling** (Reflectly, Notion AI): "What was one good thing today?"
- **Digital Detox Bots** (Focus AI, StayFree): Track and reduce screen time.
- **Voice Reminders:** "Alexa, remind me to stretch every hour."
- **AI Alarm Playlists:** Start your day with energizing music using Spotify AI.

Bonus Hack: Use ChatGPT to create a daily affirmation like: "I am focused, calm, and ready to learn."

7. Mental Health in the AI Era – Tips for Teens

AI is helpful, but:
- Don't compare yourself with AI-generated perfection.
- Use AI to improve, not to compete or escape from feelings.
- Talk to real people (teachers, parents, counselors) when feeling low.

Golden Rule: AI can guide your wellness—but only you can choose to be well.

Wellness Toolkit – Build Your AI-Based Self-Care Routine

Time	Activity	AI Tool Suggestion
6:30 AM	Wake up smart	Sleep Cycle
7:00 AM	Morning affirmation	ChatGPT / Alexa
8:00 AM	Healthy breakfast log	MyFitnessPal
12:00 PM	Drink water reminder	WaterMinder
5:00 PM	Workout or walk	Nike App / Fitbod
9:00 PM	Meditation / journaling	Headspace / Reflectly
10:00 PM	Sleep tracker on	Pillow / Fitbit

Try This – My AI Wellness Plan

Create your personal wellness checklist:

- Sleep hours goal: ___
- Daily movement target (steps/minutes): ___
- Mind relaxation tool: ___
- Meal tracking: ___
- Water intake goal: ___
- Habits to build: ___

Use any AI app to support this plan and update weekly.

NEP 2020 Alignment Spotlight

This chapter promotes:

- Physical and emotional well-being as part of holistic education.
- Self-directed life skill development using digital tools.
- Balanced routine formation through tech-aided nudges.
- 21st-century competency: self-regulation, awareness, and health-conscious behavior.

Key Takeaways

• AI supports better sleep, nutrition, fitness, emotional health, and routines.

• Tools like Sleep Cycle, Wysa, Headspace, Fitbod, and Fabulous empower students to lead healthier lives.

• Build small, consistent wellness habits supported by AI nudges and insights.

• Your body and mind are your real assets—AI simply helps you protect and optimize them.

Quick Recap Quiz

Q1. Which AI app helps track your sleep patterns?

A. Canva
B. Sleep Cycle
C. Grammarly
D. Google Earth

Q2. What does Wysa help with?

A. Grammar checking
B. Emotional wellness
C. Workout planning
D. Translation

Q3. Which of these is a healthy AI-powered life hack?

A. Skip meals to save time
B. Play games instead of sleep
C. Use WaterMinder to track hydration
D. Use AI to replace exercise

Answers: Q1 – B, Q2 – B, Q3 – C

Chapter 11

How to Use AI Tools the Right Way

Learning Objectives

By the end of this chapter, you will:

• Understand the ethical use of AI in learning, creativity, and daily life.
• Recognize the risks of misuse, plagiarism, and over-dependence on AI.
• Learn about digital responsibility, data privacy, and algorithmic bias.
• Explore how to build a respectful, human-first approach to technology.
• Create your own AI Responsibility Pledge as a student.

Why Talk About Responsibility?

AI is a powerful tool. It can help you:

• Write essays,
• Create presentations,
• Plan your time,

- Organize your wellness,
- Learn new things fast.

But power comes with responsibility.

AI is not magic—it's a machine trained on human-made data.
How you use it defines whether it becomes a friend, a crutch, or a risk.

In this chapter, we will learn how to use AI responsibly, ethically, and thoughtfully, in line with NEP 2020's goal of developing mindful digital citizens.

1. AI Misuse in Schools: What's the Problem?

Using AI is not cheating—but how you use it matters.

× Unethical Uses of AI:
- Copy-pasting ChatGPT essays without understanding.
- Using AI to solve exam papers during online assessments.
- Taking credit for AI-generated art or writing in competitions.
- Using AI for bullying, fake news, or creating deepfakes.

Consequences:
- School penalties (zero marks, disqualification).
- Missed learning opportunities.
- Reduced creativity and thinking skills.
- Unfair advantage over peers.

Quote: "When you let AI do your work, you miss the chance to grow your brain."

2. Ethical Ways to Use AI as a Student

Use AI as a collaborator, not a substitute.

Task	Ethical Use	Unethical Use
Essay Writing	Ask AI for outline ideas	Submitting AI-generated content as-is
Presentations	Use AI design templates, add your research	Using pre-made slides blindly
Research	Summarize articles, check multiple sources	Copy-paste without citation
Study Help	Explain tough concepts in simple words	Letting AI do the entire homework
Creative Work	Use AI to spark imagination, then personalize	Submit unedited AI artwork

NEP 2020 Link: Encourages responsible tech use and original thinking.

3. Don't Let AI Think For You

AI can be smart—but your brain is smarter.

Risks of Over-Dependence:
- You lose touch with real thinking.
- You stop practicing grammar, math, or analysis.
- You struggle in exams where AI isn't allowed.
- Your confidence goes down.

Build Healthy Habits:
- Use AI to check, not create everything.
- Try answering yourself first—then ask AI.
- Always review and rewrite in your own voice.

Tip: Treat AI like a study buddy, not a shortcut.

4. Protect Your Data and Privacy

AI tools often collect data to improve performance. But not all tools are safe.

Dos and Don'ts:

• ✓ Use AI tools from trusted platforms (Google, OpenAI, Canva, etc.).

• ✓ Read privacy settings before signing up.

• ✓ Use school ID or anonymous sign-ins for public tools.

• ✗ Don't share personal info like phone number, address, passwords.

• ✗ Don't upload sensitive documents to unknown apps.

Examples of Data Risks:

• A free AI photo tool saves your image without permission.

• A chatbot stores your chat history and shares it with companies.

Golden Rule: If you wouldn't share it with a stranger, don't share it with AI.

5. Understanding Bias in AI

AI is trained on data made by humans—and humans have biases.

What is AI Bias?

AI may:

• Suggest wrong facts.

• Give unfair responses.

• Reflect stereotypes from the internet.

Example:

Ask an AI: "Show me an image of a doctor."

If it shows only men, that's a bias. Real doctors come in all genders.

What You Can Do:

• Always cross-check AI responses.

• Be aware of cultural, gender, and social fairness.
• Don't believe AI is always right—it's not.

Critical Thinking Tip: Use your judgment, not just AI's output.

6. AI and Plagiarism – Know the Line

Plagiarism is using someone else's ideas, words, or images without credit. That includes AI-generated content.

Can AI-written text be plagiarized?
Yes—if:
• You submit it as fully your own.
• You don't review or personalize it.
• You copy from one AI and paste into a project.

Safe Practices:
• Rewrite and edit in your tone.
• Cite AI tools when used heavily.
• Add a note like:

"This presentation was designed using Canva AI. Content was edited and finalized by [Your Name]."

7. AI Deepfakes, Misinformation & Scams

What's the Danger?
• Deepfake videos can impersonate teachers or celebrities.
• Fake news generated by AI can spread panic.
• AI-generated scams can steal money or information.

How to Stay Safe:
• Double-check facts from official sources.
• Don't believe screenshots or "AI-created" quotes without proof.
• Never click on suspicious links from unknown bots or messages.

Remember: AI can create illusions. Be a truth-seeker, not a click-believer.

8. Digital Etiquette – The AI Age Manners

In a world full of AI chats and bots, your digital behavior matters.

Dos:
• Be polite to AI chatbots.
• Don't troll or spam AI systems.
• Give feedback when an AI gets something wrong.
• Help others learn about ethical AI.

Don'ts:
• Use AI to mock, impersonate, or attack others.
• Post fake or AI-altered images/videos without context.

Future-Ready Skill: Be a responsible digital citizen with good online manners.

9. The Student AI Responsibility Pledge

Repeat after me:
I will use AI as a tool to learn, not to cheat.
I will protect my privacy and think before I click.
I will check facts, cite sources, and use my own voice.
I will never use AI to harm, lie, or mislead others.
I will be kind, curious, and ethical in the digital world.

Try This – Your Responsible AI Checklist

✓ I read and edited any AI-generated content.
✓ I gave credit where needed.
✓ I used AI for support, not for shortcuts.

✓ I avoided sharing personal info.
✓ I cross-checked facts.
✓ I used trusted tools.
✓ I didn't misuse AI in assignments or competitions.
✓ I learned something new—not just fast.

Score yourself:
7–8 ✓ = AI Champion
5–6 = On Track
< 5 × = Time to reflect and improve!

NEP 2020 Alignment Spotlight

This chapter supports:

- Ethical digital use and digital fluency.
- Development of critical thinking and originality.
- Safe and responsible student behavior in tech environments.
- Plagiarism awareness and prevention strategies.

Key Takeaways

- Use AI to learn smarter—not to cheat, lie, or escape effort.
- Protect your data, question results, and stay fair in competitions.
- Know that AI isn't perfect—it carries bias, risk, and misinformation.
- NEP 2020 wants you to be a thinking student, not a copying one.
- Respect technology, use it wisely, and lead by example.

Abeer's Tech Tip
Never submit AI-generated work without editing it in your own voice.
Amaara Asks
If AI makes a mistake, who is responsible — the machine or the human?

Quick Recap Quiz

Q1. What is a responsible use of AI?
A. Submitting AI-written homework as-is
B. Asking AI to explain a topic, then writing it yourself
C. Copy-pasting chatbot answers in tests
D. Using AI to prank your classmates

Q2. What should you do before sharing personal data with an AI app?
A. Trust it
B. Ask a friend
C. Check privacy settings and platform reputation
D. Assume it's safe if it's free

Q3. What is the best way to avoid AI plagiarism?
A. Change 1–2 words
B. Use the text without edits
C. Acknowledge AI assistance and rewrite in your voice
D. Delete citations

Answers: Q1 – B, Q2 – C, Q3 – C

Chapter 12

The Future of AI in Your Career

Learning Objectives

By the end of this chapter, you will:

- Understand how AI is transforming careers across every field.
- Explore emerging job roles and AI-supported professions.
- Learn how to prepare for an AI-powered future using 21st-century skills.
- Identify digital skills that complement AI.
- Create a roadmap for your dream career with AI as a collaborator.

The Future Is Not Far—It's Here

Just 10 years ago, hardly anyone imagined:

- Talking to a chatbot that writes essays,
- Getting art and music from a machine,
- Receiving workout, study, and career plans from an app.

Now, AI is everywhere—and it's not going away.

AI isn't taking all the jobs. But students who understand and use AI will take the best ones.

This chapter is your career compass, helping you navigate the exciting world of AI-powered professions, smart skills, and future-readiness.

1. Will AI Take My Job?

This is the most common question—and the answer is: No, but it will change how jobs work.

Three Things to Remember:
1. AI will replace repetitive and rule-based tasks (data entry, basic reports, etc.).
2. AI will assist professionals, not replace them, in fields like teaching, medicine, law, and design.
3. New jobs will be created—many that don't even exist yet.

The future belongs to those who can combine human creativity + emotional intelligence + smart use of AI.

2. How AI Will Change Existing Careers

Let's look at how common career paths are evolving with AI:

Career Field	AI Transformation Example
Medicine	AI diagnostics, robotic surgery assistants, health chatbots
Education	AI tutors, personalized learning tools, smart assessments
Law	AI contract readers, legal research assistants

Engineering	AI-based simulations, predictive maintenance tools
Journalism	AI-assisted news writing, fact-checking tools
Finance	AI fraud detection, investment bots, budgeting assistants
Agriculture	AI crop health monitoring, smart irrigation systems
Marketing	AI ad targeting, content creation, brand bots
Environment	AI climate modeling, disaster prediction tools

Reflection Prompt: What's your dream career? Look up how AI is being used in that field today.

3. Emerging Careers in the AI Age

Some new job roles being created due to AI include:

Job Title	What They Do
AI Prompt Engineer	Designs smart queries and inputs to make AI work better
Data Scientist	Finds patterns in big data and trains AI models
AI Ethics Officer	Ensures AI is fair, unbiased, and used responsibly
Human-AI Interaction Designer	Creates user-friendly interfaces between humans and machines
Automation Specialist	Uses AI to improve efficiency in industries
AI Trainer	Teaches AI to recognize correct vs incorrect outputs
XR Developer (AI + VR/AR)	Creates immersive experiences using AI and extended reality

Pro Tip: These careers often don't require just tech knowledge—they value curiosity, communication, problem-solving, and ethical thinking.

4. Non-Tech Students Can Thrive with AI

You don't have to become a coder to work with AI.
If you are into arts, commerce, humanities, or social science, you can:

- Use AI to create content and campaigns.
- Study social impact of AI in psychology or sociology.
- Explore ethical challenges of AI in philosophy or law.
- Build data stories in economics or journalism.

Quote: "AI won't replace you—but someone using AI will outperform you."

5. Must-Have Digital Skills for the Future

Whether you want to become a doctor, designer, or data scientist, you'll need these core skills:

Skill	Why It Matters
Digital Literacy	Understand how digital tools and AI work
Critical Thinking	Analyze AI outputs for bias and accuracy
Communication Skills	Explain complex ideas clearly (AI can't do empathy!)
Creativity	Combine human imagination with AI suggestions
Collaboration	Work in teams, often across locations and time zones
Data Fluency	Read graphs, interpret numbers, use basic analytics

Ethical Awareness	Use AI responsibly and make fair decisions

Try This: Take a basic course in any of these areas on Coursera, Google Skillshop, or Khan Academy.

6. AI Tools to Explore Careers

You can start exploring your career options using AI tools designed for students:

Tools to Try:
• Career Coach AI (Unschool) – Personalized learning paths for different goals.
• AI Resume Builders (Enhancv, Teal) – Help craft resumes using AI prompts.
• LinkedIn Learning + AI – Suggests courses based on your interest.
• Notion AI – Build a career plan dashboard.
• Internshala AI Job Guide – Matches internships to your skill profile.

• **ChatGPT – Ask:**
"What are 5 careers in psychology that use AI?"
or
"How do I become an ethical hacker after 12th grade?"

Activity: Use ChatGPT to explore a career path by typing:
"I love storytelling and technology. What careers suit me in the AI era?"

7. From Student to Future-Ready Professional

Step-by-Step Plan:
1. **Discover:** Explore your interests (what do you enjoy doing?)
2. **Connect:** Match interests to career fields using AI tools or mentors

3. **Skill Up:** Start with one digital/AI-related skill (e.g., Canva, Python, SEO)
4. **Create:** Build a portfolio—slides, blogs, short videos, school projects
5. **Reflect:** Journal your learning path using Notion or Google Docs
6. **Share:** Start a small YouTube, LinkedIn, or blog page
7. **Stay Curious**: Follow AI news, trends, student communities (like AI4Youth)

Tip: It's not about being the best. It's about being adaptable, curious, and ethical.

Real Teen Voices

"I used Canva AI to design event posters for our school. Now I want to study marketing and media." – Riya, Class 11

"ChatGPT helped me prepare for my commerce project and inspired me to start a finance YouTube channel." – Arjun, Class 10

"My dream is to become a lawyer. AI helps me summarize cases and analyze news faster." – Tanya, Class 12

NEP 2020 Alignment Spotlight

This chapter supports:

- Exposure to emerging technologies.
- Career awareness and skilling.
- Multidisciplinary approach (AI across all subjects).
- Self-directed and inquiry-based learning.
- Development of future-ready competencies.

Key Takeaways

- AI will not eliminate jobs—it will reshape them.
- New roles are emerging across every stream—arts, science,

commerce, and vocational fields.

- Start now by building smart, digital, and human skills.
- Use AI tools to explore careers, build portfolios, and learn.
- The future belongs to curious learners who know how to use AI ethically and creatively.

Abeer's Tech Tip

Start building a small portfolio now — even 3 projects show more initiative than 10 certificates.

Amaara Asks

Will AI create more opportunities than it replaces?

Quick Recap Quiz

Q1. Which job is emerging due to AI?

A. AI Prompt Engineer
B. Typewriter Mechanic
C. Coal Miner
D. CD Designer

Q2. What's a good way to explore careers with AI?

A. Ask AI to choose for you and follow blindly
B. Use tools like ChatGPT and Career Coach AI to match your interests
C. Copy your friend's plan
D. Avoid using AI at all

Q3. Which skill is NOT a future-ready competency?

A. Digital literacy
B. Collaboration
C. Memorization of textbook lines
D. Critical thinking

Answers: Q1 – A, Q2 – B, Q3 – C

Bonus Section

Master Directory of AI Tools for Students

Why This Directory?

This master directory is your ready reference list of beginner-friendly, NEP 2020–aligned,

AI-powered tools designed for:

- Smarter studying
- Creative thinking
- Better time management
- Enhanced productivity
- Health and wellness
- Ethical digital living

Each tool includes:

- Name
- Category

• Use Case
• Website Link
Use it to build your AI learning dashboard, pick tools for your projects, or simply explore what suits your goals and style.

✓ **How to Use the Table**
• Explore one tool per week
• Test it with a real task (assignment, project, habit, hobby)
• Add your own notes in Notion or Google Docs
• Update it as AI evolves!

A. Study & Research Helpers

Tool Name	Category	Use Case	Link
ChatGPT	Chat Assistant	Ask questions, summarize topics, brainstorm ideas	chat.openai.com
Claude	Chat Assistant	Long document summarizer and writing help	claude.ai
Elicit	Research Assistant	Find insights from academic papers	elicit.org
Scholarcy	Summarizer	Extract key points from PDFs, academic texts	scholarcy.com
Mindgrasp	Study Aid	Generate notes, quizzes, and audio summaries	mindgrasp.ai
Notion AI	All-in-One Tool	Study planner, content creator, and knowledge hub	notion.so

Caktus AI	Study Assistant	Subject-based tutoring, writing, and research support	caktus.ai
Tactiq	Meeting Notes	Transcribe and summarize Google Meet, Zoom classes	tactiq.io

B. Writing, Reading & Content Tools

Tool Name	Category	Use Case	Link
Grammarly	Writing Assistant	Spelling, grammar, and clarity checking	grammarly.com
Jenni AI	Essay Writer	Paragraph suggestions, structure help, citations	jenni.ai
Writesonic	AI Writing Tool	Blogs, essays, story writing with templates	writesonic.com
ChatDOC	PDF Reader	Ask questions and summarize from PDFs	chatdoc.com
PDFgear AI	Summarizer/ Reader	Highlight and summarize PDF content	pdfgear.com
Readwise Reader	Reading Organizer	Smart reading, highlighting, note syncing	readwise.io

Quillbot	Paraphraser	Rewriting and rephrasing content in better language	quillbot.com

C. Productivity & Time Management

Tool Name	Category	Use Case	Link
Reclaim AI	Calendar Assistant	Block time for study, rest, and planning	reclaim.ai
Clockwise	Smart Scheduler	Sync school, home, and project schedules	getclockwise.com
Motion	Task Manager	Prioritize tasks with AI-suggested schedules	usemotion.com
SkedPal	AI Planner	Plans your to-do list based on deadlines	skedpal.com
Twos App	Smart Organizer	Collect notes, tasks, and ideas in one place	twosapp.com

D. Creativity, Design & Presentation

Tool Name	Category	Use Case	Link
Canva AI	Design Tool	Posters, slides, resumes with AI design help	canva.com
Tome	Presentation Builder	Auto-create presentations and visuals	tome.app
Gamma	Slide Generator	Stylish slides with storytelling prompts	gamma.app
Midjourney	Image Generator	Create images from text prompts (via Discord)	midjourney.com
Feyn	Visual Notes	Turn concepts into visuals/diagrams	feyn.app
OpusClip	Video Editor	Convert long videos into short viral clips	opus.pro
Synthesia	Video Generator	Make videos with avatars and voice-overs	synthesia.io

E. Communication, Listening & Language

Tool Name	Category	Use Case	Link
Siri / Alexa / Google Assistant	Voice Assistants	Set reminders, ask questions, get translations	Built-in on devices

Speechify	Voice Reader	Listen to PDFs, textbooks, and webpages	speechify.com
Play.ht	Audio Generator	Convert text to audio in human-like voice	play.ht
ElevenLabs	Voice Cloner	Create natural-sounding voice content	elevenlabs.io
DeepL Translate	Translator	Translate long text with high accuracy	deepl.com
Duolingo	Language Learning	Learn new languages using gamified AI tools	duolingo.com

F. Health, Habits & Lifestyle

Tool Name	Category	Use Case	Link
Sleep Cycle	Smart Alarm	Track sleep quality and wake you at best time	sleepcycle.com
ElliQ	Wellness Assistant	For elderly companionship and motivation	elliq.com
SmartKit	All-in-One Tracker	AI-based reminders, health tips, goals	smartkit.app

Beatleap	Mood-based Music	Auto-mix music and videos based on energy level	beatleapapp.com

G. Discovery, Web Search & Knowledge

Tool Name	Category	Use Case	Link
Merlin AI	Web Helper	Chat with websites, summarize pages	getmerlin.in
You.com	AI Search Engine	Chat and search with summarized answers	you.com
Perplexity	AI Answer Engine	Ask questions, get cited answers from real sources	perplexity.ai
Consensus	Science Search	Find scientific research papers and evidence	consensus.app

Final Notes & Updates

This directory is:

- **Living** – update it every month!
- **Learn-by-doing** – try real tasks
- **Customizable** – pick what suits your needs

Save this list in your Notion or Google Drive and build your own AI Toolkit for Life.

GLOSSARY

A beginner-friendly guide to important terms used in this book

Term	Definition
AI (Artificial Intelligence)	The simulation of human-like intelligence by machines that can think, learn, and solve problems.
Algorithm	A set of instructions or rules given to a computer to perform a task or solve a problem.
Machine Learning	A type of AI where machines learn from data and improve their performance without being directly programmed.
Generative AI	AI that can create new content like text, images, music, or videos (e.g., ChatGPT, Midjourney).
Narrow AI	AI trained to do one specific task very well (e.g., face recognition, voice assistants).
General AI	Hypothetical AI that can perform any intellectual task a human can do (not yet achieved).
AI Agent	A system that perceives its environment and acts to achieve a goal, often using sensors, logic, and feedback.
Chatbot	A computer program designed to simulate conversation with human users, especially online.
Virtual Assistant	AI-powered tools like Siri or Alexa that help users with voice commands or tasks.
Prompt	The instruction or message you give to an AI tool to generate a specific output.

Data	Raw information (like numbers, words, or clicks) that AI systems use to learn and make decisions.
Digital Literacy	The ability to find, evaluate, use, and create information using digital tools.
Plagiarism	Copying someone else's work or ideas without giving credit — considered unethical and dishonest.
Bias (in AI)	When an AI system makes unfair decisions due to errors in the data or its design.
Automation	The use of technology to perform tasks without human input, often making things faster and more efficient.
Productivity	Getting more done in less time, often with the help of tools like AI planners, reminders, or organizers.
XR (Extended Reality)	A combination of virtual reality (VR), augmented reality (AR), and mixed reality (MR) technologies.
Digital Footprint	The trail of data you leave online when you browse, post, or use apps.
Ethical Use of AI	Using AI responsibly, without cheating, harming others, or spreading misinformation.

BOOK SUMMARY

AI Unlocked: The Student's Guide to Smart Living, Learning & Limitless Productivity

This student-friendly guide introduces teenagers to the exciting and fast-changing world of Artificial Intelligence (AI). Written with the vision of the NEP 2020 and NCF 2023, the book empowers Indian students in Grades 9–12 to become smart, ethical, and future-ready learners.

Key Highlights:

• **Chapters 1–4** introduce the 5Ws of AI (What, Why, Where, When, Who), its types, and how it connects to student life.

• **Chapters 5–10 offer real-world AI tools that can enhance:**

- o Studying and note-making
- o Time and task management
- o Writing and research
- o Creativity and design
- o Voice, language, and communication
- o Health, habits, and personal routines

• **Chapter 11** emphasizes digital responsibility and the ethical use of AI—no cheating, no misuse.

• **Chapter 12** helps students explore the future of careers in AI, from tech to humanities, and guides them in building the skills needed to thrive.

• The Bonus Section features a detailed, categorized Master

Directory of AI Tools for Students, with descriptions and clickable links for hands-on learning.

Learning Outcomes:

• Develop 21st-century skills: critical thinking, digital fluency, collaboration, and self-directed learning.
• Learn to use AI not just for fun or curiosity—but to become more efficient, creative, and confident in academics and life.
• Build awareness of AI ethics, safety, and privacy in a connected world.
• Plan for future careers using real AI applications and tools available today.

NEP 2020 Alignment:

• Competency-based, real-world learning
• Exposure to emerging technologies
• Multidisciplinary integration
• Ethical awareness and digital literacy
• Career readiness and self-regulation